FEMINISM:
A RESEARCH AND CONTENT
WORKBOOK

FEMINISM:
A RESEARCH AND CONTENT WORKBOOK

Susan Louise Peterson, Ph.D.

Editorial Inquiries:
International Scholars Publications
7831 Woodmont Avenue, #345
Bethesda, MD 20814
website: www.interscholars.com
To order: (800) 55-PUBLISH

Dedicated
-once again to Alan,
my best friend and marriage partner

TABLE OF CONTENTS

FOREWORD

Susan Louise Peterson's *Feminism: A Research and Content Workbook* is a thought-provoking, discussion-generating workbook and a useful guide to the concepts of feminism. Teachers of students at all educational levels will find something of use in this practical text. It does an outstanding job of converting feminist educational theory into experiential exercises in which students are asked to blend the personal, political and theoretical into the practical aspects of feminism. Who better to provide us with this very pragmatic book than Susan Louise Peterson? She holds a master's degree in human relations and a doctorate in family relations and child development; and she has taught at all educational levels from pre-school to the university. Susan is a woman who "walks the walk"--she truly does know what works for teachers because she is engaged in teaching all levels both the young child and the adult learner. Susan has also included a chapter which tells readers how to go about getting their own work published. This is an important contribution to the idea that women's studies is a communal work---we all have ideas which deserve sharing and Susan tells us how to go about getting our work printed.

This useful book comes at a time when it is sorely needed. Since the first women's studies program began at San Diego State University in 1969-70, women's studies has continued the vital work of making the world a better place for both men and women. Yet after thirty years of working at this world changing labor, we find ourselves at an important crossroads. The conservative right has committed enormous resources to reversing the progress that women have gained. The only way to curb this backlash is to meet the opposition with a renewed struggle for improving women's and girls' lives. We must help others understand that this battle is not simply a battle for equity, it is a fight for human rights.

Feminism: A Research and Content Workbook makes an important contribution to helping us change the way we view women's and girls' place in the world. Use the phrases as prompts for writing journal entries. Use the exercises in a classroom, a girls scout troop, a consciousness raising group, a spirituality group, a reading group---in fact, this workbook could be used anywhere--- including around dinner table. The possibilities are endless. Buy and use this useful book---buy another and give it to a friend who teaches.

Sonia Johnson reminds us, "We must remember that one determined person can make a significant difference and that a small group of determined people can change the course of history." Our work awaits us.

Professor Glenda Hufnagel, Assistant Director-
Department of Human Relations Advanced Program
University of Oklahoma

PREFACE

There has never been more need in history than the present for the investigation, and an analysis of, the concepts and myths surrounding feminism. This is apparent when considering contemporary society's dynamics and its pervasive impact on the individual. Lack of critical thinking about the concept of feminism has significantly detrimental consequences. These consequences include the capacity to erode individual self-esteem, to devalue the feminine experience, and undermine women's potential for personal and professional achievement. Furthermore, these outcomes not only directly impact the well-being of women, but also of the individuals they interact with.

Intrapersonally, it is important to specifically determine personal values, ethics, and boundaries. This requires internal searching to understand what we each hold as truths as a human being for ourselves and for others. Clearly there is value in examining our self-concept (the relatively stable set of perceptions we hold of our self). We need to probe the governing rules we each have learned to live by, to survive by, through social and family conditioning. As individuals, it is important to discern our tolerance levels for ambiguity and the employment of power and control over others.

Interpersonally, we continuously influence, and are influenced, by our relationships. Through the uses of verbal and non-verbal communication processes, we impact each other intentionally and unintentionally. There are no areas in life so sacred as to be left untouched- family relationships, intimate love relationships, friendships, occupational dynamics, and organizational ties are all affected. Our attitudes about feminism in relationship to: gender role behaviors and activities, cultural and ethnic diversity, stereotyping, and conflict management directly effect the perceptions others have of us, thereby directly impacting the quality of each relationship. Dilemmas and their subsequent pain are created when individual belief systems collide.

I encourage you to consider the issues of feminism on an increasingly larger scale as you develop greater personal insight into your relationship with feminism. Is this an issue of 'good vs. bad' or 'right vs. wrong'? Is the concept of feminism inherently desirable/undesirable? What are the results of presenting a feminist attitude from a sociological perspective? What can individuals do to facilitate enhanced regard and respect for the 'humanness' in each of us?

Telisa L. Clevenger, Adjunct Professor
Hank Greenspun School of Communication/College of Urban Affairs
University of Nevada Las Vegas
Operations Manager, VIDIAD

ACKNOWLEDGMENTS

There are many people to thank who have helped and encouraged me to gain a greater awareness of women's issues. A special thank you goes to Glenda Hufnagel from my alma mater, the University of Oklahoma for her words of encouragement and support. Telisa Clevenger was also very insightful with her thoughts of feminism and responded to my requests in a timely manner. I cannot forget to thank my husband, Alan who overwhelms me daily with his friendship and love. Thanks to Nicola Noll for her helpful editorial suggestions. I would also like to thank Dr. Robert West for his continued support at International Scholars Publications.

INTRODUCTION

Much of the confusion of feminism stems from three major areas. First, problems stem from communication about the issues of feminism. For example, in some relationships, a person may not listen to a woman's concerns and may respond emotionally without weighing the issues that impact her life. Second, since feminism addresses broad issues, there are many parts of it that are left up to individual interpretation. Each individual's background is so unique with different social situations and family backgrounds that each person's view of feminism differs. Third, the concerns of feminism are confusing because they are in a state of change. As women mature and grow in their life experiences, changes occur that cause their views of feminism to alter. This book is written to help increase the awareness and understanding of feminist issues through a variety of writing and discussion projects. It is hoped that by analyzing and discussing these concerns the confusion of feminism will be lessened and that women and men will communicate more effectively about these important issues in their lives.

Writers interested in the field of women's studies are faced with challenges in getting their works published. They must search diligently to find publishers who share an interest in their ideas about feminism and women's issues. Writers in this field are faced with three major challenges in getting women's studies manuscripts published. First, many women's studies presses are small and on extremely tight budgets. These presses are often bombarded with numerous manuscripts, but can only accept a handful for publication. Second, women's studies presses may specialize in a particular area, such as the history of women, and are limited to women's studies manuscripts on that particular topic. Third, there are still misconceptions about the ideas of feminism and the issues facing women.

Publishers may not always share the views of some women's studies writers. Despite these challenges, there are still an array of opportunities to write in the area of women's studies. This book is written to encourage women's studies writers by sharing practical advice about the publishing world and provide a comprehensive compilation of phrases for those writing in the area of women's studies.

CHAPTER ONE

SCENARIOS AND DISCUSSION QUESTIONS

The scenarios presented in this chapter are based on my observations of real life experiences of women and men. Oddly enough, some of the same relationship and communication types of problems that existed ten or twenty years ago are still concerns today. There are discussion questions after each scenario to identify the problem areas and analyze the meanings or reactions to the scenarios. It is hoped that class members will share a variety of perspectives about the scenarios. The students will have opportunities to give feedback to one another about the issues that are unique to each scenario.

SCENARIO #1

"DON'T CALL ME A FEMINIST"

Abby never wanted to be associated with anything connected to the word feminist. She knew it was not very popular idea among her college friends. Abby was a very competitive person and liked to be treated fairly in all things. She decided to write a research comparison paper for a business class on pay salaries of female and male office managers. Abby made a class presentation and she emphasized the pay salaries of females and males were not equal. There were even some major differences in female and male managers salaries when they had similar educational degrees and work experience. After her presentation, other students in the class could make comments and ask questions to the presenter. One young college student made the comment to Abby that, "You must be a feminist to write such a paper." Abby responded back, "Don't call me a feminist." She was upset that someone in the class labeled her as a feminist because she pointed out pay inequities between females and males in her research paper.

DISCUSSION QUESTIONS
FOR SCENARIO #1

1. What issue was important to Abby in the scenario?

2. Why do you think Abby resented being called the word feminist?

3. In your opinion, was the college student's reaction to Abby's paper reasonable or a narrow minded view? Why?

4. Do you think Abby was having an internal conflict about the word feminist? Yes or No? Explain your answer.

5. How could Abby gain a better understanding of what feminism means?

6. Some young college women do not want to be associated with the word feminist. Why do you think they are so negative about this word?

7. What is your definition of the word feminism?

8. Do you think feminism is a controversial topic? Yes or No? Why?

9. What do you view as the successes of the feminist or women's movement?

10. In your viewpoint, what are some failures of the feminist or women's movement?

11. Do you think Abby's attitude about being a feminist is typical among college women today? Yes or No? Why?

12. Look at your family background. How were women treated in your family? Give an example.

SCENARIO #2

"I DO NOT WANT TO BE A SUPERWOMAN"

Jane and Craig started dating in a college. Jane fell in love with Craig instantly because he was so supportive of her college education and career potential. Shortly after their marriage, Craig encouraged Jane to work. He appreciated her income for the monthly expenses. Jane, however has become discouraged. She is frustrated because not only does she work full-time, but she also does most of the household chores. Her evenings are spent doing the laundry, grocery shopping, cleaning the house, and cooking dinner each night. Jane thinks, "I do not want to be a superwoman." She just wants some help with the household chores. They have a positive relationship and Jane does not want to rock the boat by saying how she really feels about the situation.

Many young college and career women would probably never imagine that this problem still exists. The fact that women work does not change the fact that household chores still exist. What does change is how the responsibilities of housework are distributed between the spouses in a dual career marriage.

DISCUSSION QUESTIONS
FOR SCENARIO #2

1. Can you identify the problem Jane faced in the scenario?

2. What are some of the consequences Jane might face by not expressing her feelings to Craig?

3. What major responsibilities were stressing Jane?

4. How do you think Craig might respond if Jane were honest with him about the situation?

5. Pretend you are Jane's best friend. What advice would you give her to help her through this difficult time?

6. Does Jane need professional help to solve her problem? Yes or No? Explain your answer.

7. What are some common problems related to housework that married couples face?

8. How could the couple in the scenario better organize their lifestyle to address this problem?

9. What values were important to Jane in the scenario?

10. What do you think is the best way for Jane to approach Craig about this problem?

11. What term would best describe the couple's problem? For example, is it a communication problem, a relationship problem, or another type of problem?

12. What are some possible solutions to Jane and Craig's problem?

SCENARIO #3

WHERE WERE YOU?

Judy was an extremely overweight first year school teacher. She was engaged to James, a very independent store manager who still liked to spend most of his time with his buddies. Judy and James called each other every weekend as they discussed their wedding plans. One weekend Judy called James several times and could not locate him. She began to worry that he might have been injured in a car wreck. When she finally spoke to him on Monday morning, he gave her a flimsy excuse that the cat knocked the phone off the hook all weekend. Judy thinks he was out partying with his friends. When Judy shared the incident in a graduate college communications course, her professor encouraged her to talk with her fiancee and be open with him about the incident. Judy responded to her professor by saying, "I could never do that because he would leave me and I would never see him again." Judy never talked with James about the incident before their wedding.

DISCUSSION QUESTIONS
FOR SCENARIO #3

1. What problem did Judy face in the scenario?

2. Where did the communication breakdown begin in this problem?

3. Why do you think the professor and Judy came up with such different solutions for working out her problem?

4. Do you feel Judy's weight problem had an impact on her self-confidence to discuss the concern with her fiancee? Yes or No? Explain why.

5. If Judy had told James how she really felt and he responded angrily what could she have done?

6. What problems have you experienced that are similar to the one Judy faced in the scenario? Give an example.

7. Do you think Judy and James could help improve their relationship through premarital counseling? Yes or No? Explain why.

8. What would you advise your sister to do if she was having the same conflict as Judy did in the scenario?

9. Why do you think Judy had such a low self-confidence to confront this relatively simple problem?

10. How can the couple come to a compromise and improve their relationship?

11. What would you predict will happen next to Judy?

12. What steps could Judy use to prevent this problem in the future?

SCENARIO #4

IT IS A WOMAN'S JOB

Kathy earns a living for her family. She works full-time in an accounting firm and makes an excellent salary. Her husband Lee is unemployed and they have an infant son. Kathy is frustrated because Lee refuses to help take care of the baby while she is at work. Lee demands that Kathy take the baby to the sitter every day, even when he is at home sitting idle in front of the television. He also has extravagant tastes and buys expensive clothes, shoes and hobby collectibles. Lee feels that because he is the man of the house, and he should control the finances. He cut up several of Kathy's credit cards one day while she was at work.

Lee also refuses to cook meals for Kathy because he thinks, "It is a woman's job." They had a huge argument the other day because Lee was upset that Kathy came home from work thirty minutes later than usual. Kathy could not understand his frustration because she is in a high stress job and is the principle wage earner of the family.

DISCUSSION QUESTIONS
FOR SCENARIO #4

1. What impact did Kathy's career have on the relationship?

2. How would you define the relationship problem in the scenario?

3. What are some possible explanations for Lee's behavior?

4. How would you explain the differences in Kathy and Lee's point of view?

5. What could Kathy do to facilitate a more positive relationship with Lee?

6. Put yourself in Kathy's situation. How would you respond to a man who talked to you this way?

7. How did each partner interpret the problem?

8. Why do you think this situation happened?

9. What resources are available to help this couple improve their situation?

10. What attitudes did Lee have that made the situation uncomfortable?

11. What topics could be included in a women's studies course that could help the couple improve their situation?

12. How could the couple enhance their relationship?

SCENARIO #5

STAY AT HOME PARENTS

Janet, James and Libby were all stay at home parents, but their situations were totally different. Janet was a single parent who was working a minimum wage job. She quit her job to stay at home with her children because it was cheaper to stay at home than to afford the day care center. James was a stay at home parent who worked out of his home to spend more time with his children. He had a job involving phone work and setting appointments from his home. Libby was a mother who decided to stay at home with the children because she was tired of the rat race. Her spouse had an excellent job and they could financially afford for Libby to stay at home. Libby made a choice that it was best to stay at home with the children while they were young. Stay at home parents come in many different forms. Their financial and family situations may greatly vary and their reasons for staying at home may be misunderstood by those unfamiliar with their personal situations.

DISCUSSION QUESTIONS
FOR SCENARIO #5

1. Did Janet have any other choices than to stay at home? Yes or No? Explain your answer.

2. What are some community resources that might be available to help Janet?

3. How would you contrast Janet's situation as a stay at home parent with Libby's situation?

4. How do you think people in your community would view James as a stay at home parent?

5. Do you think society views women and men differently in their roles as stay at home parents? Yes or No? Why or why not?

6. Would a person's financial situation and choice to stay at home have an impact on the enjoyment as a stay at home parent. Yes or No? Explain your answer.

7. If you were director of a women's center, how would you help a woman who did not want to stay at home and wanted to get a job?

8. What is the major reason that James chose to stay at home?

9. Think of someone that you have known who has been a stay at home parent. How would you describe him or her?

10. What are some advantages of being a stay at home parent?

11. Can you describe some of the weaknesses or disadvantages a person might experience being a stay at home parent?

12. What creative approaches could stay at home parents use to avoid becoming bored in their positions?

SCENARIO #6

THE ALUMNI

Martha, a recent college graduate, became very excited when she was invited to join an alumni organization from the college she had attended. She looked forward to networking with many of the female college graduates that would now be in successful careers. Martha was living in a major metropolitan area so she assumed that this would be a great organization to find positive female role models. Martha went to several of the meetings, but became discouraged because the alumni club centered more around men, football and watching games at a local bar. The wives of the men in the organization often did not attend the meetings. Martha became tired of being the only woman alumni at several events.

DISCUSSION QUESTIONS
FOR SCENARIO #6

1. What problem did Martha face in the scenario?

2. What assumptions can be made about Martha's situation?

3. Where could Martha go to find information and resources to help her identify women that could network with her?

4. Why do you think the wives of the alumni members did not attend the meetings?

5. How would you explain Martha's dilemma?

6. Does Martha have a valid reason to be discouraged about her alumni group? Yes or No? Explain your answer.

7. How might Martha learn more about women's issues and networking in her community?

8. What kind of response do you think Martha would get if she voiced her concern openly at a meeting of all men?

9. What would you predict will happen to Martha next?

10. What steps could Martha take to better her situation?

11. If Martha decides to address this situation, what will be her biggest obstacle?

12. What can alumni organizations do to involve more women in their organizations?

CHAPTER TWO

ESSAY ASSIGNMENTS

This chapter contains twenty essay starters. A brief idea is presented and students will write one page essays to discuss or describe their reactions and responses to a variety of situations related to men and women. These essays can be shared in classroom lessons to stimulate discussions and exchange life experiences. Different opinions and honest answers from students are appreciated.

OPENING THE DOOR

Mike had always been accustomed to opening the doors for women. One day he was carrying several boxes and his hands were full. A woman politely opened the door for him and his mouth fell open. He was not quite sure what to say. Write a one page essay describing your reaction to this situation.

WHO WILL WIN THE RACE?

Bobby and Beverly were six year old twins. They had been spending the day at the park with their father. He suggested that Bobby and Beverly race to the fence. Beverly won the race by a large margin because of her quick speed. Bobby could not handle the idea of his twin sister beating him in the race. He started to make up excuses for not winning the race. He said, "Beverly got a head start and she cheated." Write a one page essay describing why Bobby responded the way he did after losing the race.

THE PRETTIEST APPLICANT

Sheryl and Reba were college roommates. Sheryl was a tall, tan and attractive college student with average grades. Reba was a sort, stocky red head with excellent grades. Whenever they competed against each other, Reba noticed that Sheryl seemed to win out in each contest. Sheryl beat Reba in the cheerleader tryouts. In the student government elections, Sheryl had more votes than Reba. Even in a scholarship contest that was contingent on good academic performance, Sheryl won the scholarship over Reba. In a one page essay describe how physical beauty influences people in our society. How do you feel about this issue?

HOLIDAY SEASON

Think about a holiday you celebrated with your family. Who was responsible for organizing the celebration-a man or a woman? Describe the event in a one page essay.

SELF CONFIDENCE

Young women pursuing careers sometimes deal with issues of self confidence. Write an essay about a young woman who doubted her abilities or had a lack of self confidence about herself? Why do you think this occurred?

RELATIONSHIP PROBLEMS

Many relationships break up over issues such as who does the housework or spends the money. What do you feel is the cause of many of these problems that couples experience? In your one page essay describe some ways that men and women could improve their relationships.

WOMEN LEADERS

Describe in a one page essay what qualities make a strong woman leader.

SEXISM

Give an example of sexism that occurs in today's society. Write a one page essay describing how women should respond to sexism.

ADVICE NEEDED

In a one page essay, give some advice for a young female college graduate who wants a full time career and a positive marriage relationship.

THE WOMEN'S MOVEMENT

In a one page essay explore what comes to your mind when you hear the phrase, *The Women's Movement.*

CONTEMPORARY WOMAN

Write a one page essay and explore some of the advantages and disadvantages of being a woman in the present times.

FEMALE OR MALE

If you could chose your gender in our society, do you think it would be easier to be a female or a male? State the reasons for the gender you selected in a one page essay.

OBSTACLES FOR WOMEN

In a one page essay, describe some of the biggest obstacles women face in society.

ADMIRABLE WOMEN

Think about a woman you admire. Explain what qualities you enjoy about this admirable woman in a one page essay.

WOMEN AND ANGER

Tell a story about a time when a woman was angry with you. Did the woman have a justified reason to be angry with you? Explain your answer in a one page essay.

THE OPPOSITE SEX

Write a one page essay describing both a positive and negative experience you had with someone of the opposite sex.

BOOK CHARACTERS

Think about a book you enjoy reading. Are your favorite characters in the book male or female? Write a one page essay describing the characters and how you identify with them.

COSTUME FUN

Think back as a child when you celebrated Halloween or another holiday when you dressed up in a costume. Did you dress up as a traditional male or female character or did you have a neutral costume with no gender such as a ghost? Describe your character and why you picked the costume in a one page essay.

FRIENDSHIPS

When you were a youngster in elementary school, did you play more with friends of your same sex or the opposite sex? Describe some of your friendships in a one page essay.

DOMINATE PARENTS

Write a one page essay describing your parents or primary caretakers. Who made the household rules, your mother or your father? Which parent enforced the household rules? Were the children in the family treated differently based on their sex?

CHAPTER THREE

PARAGRAPH PROMPTS

The purpose of paragraph prompts is to encourage students to brainstorm and spontaneously write a paragraph or statements of ideas from a short phrase. This allows students to express themselves freely. It provides opportunities for students to share their feelings and experiences and to explain them to other class participants. The exchange of information will provide opportunities for students to give feedback to each other.

PARAGRAPH PROMPTS

Finish each of the prompts and write one paragraph explaining your answer.

1. Feminism means...

2. The media portrays women as...

3. The most annoying thing about men is...

4. My earliest memory of a woman in a career was...

5. The person who did most of the cooking in our household was my...

6. A major concern for older women is...

7. I feel that most television programs portray women as...

8. The most thrilling thing about being a woman or a man is...

9. When I am near someone of the opposite sex, I start to feel...

10. Adolescent girls are...

11. The person who managed the money in my family was my...

12. Violence against women happens because...

13. My mother's most admirable trait is...

14. I like to compete against...

15. The teacher I respected most was...

16. My best male friend is...

17. Dual career marriages mean...

18. In a dual career marriage, the house should be cleaned by the...

19. The grandparent that influenced me most was...

20. If I could be the son or daughter in a family, I would chose to be the...

21. Women are viewed as...

22. My favorite female television character is...

23. The most popular student in my senior high school class was...

24. I was raised by my...

25. Women leaders have...

26. Women in politics struggle with...

27. The salaries of women in professional positions are...

28. Women frustrate men because...

29. My least favorite female boss was...

30. Women make a big deal about...

31. I prefer to work for a female or a male because...

32. Women are sometimes difficult to...

33. My mother's discipline was...

34. The person who helped me with my homework was my...

35. In marriage, the woman should...

36. The major decisions in a family should be made by the...

37. A woman's most valued possession is her...

38. Equal rights mean that...

39. Women's liberation is...

40. Women's lives have improved because of...

41. Women's studies refers to...

42. Some men hate feminism because...

43. Sexism means...

44. Feminism is sometimes misunderstood because...

45. Women are more often asked to...

46. Girls in my family were not allowed to…

47. The biggest problem a woman and a man must work out in marriage is…

48. The woman who motivated me the most was…

49. A future issue for women will be...

50. The most wonderful thing about women is...

51. The one habit that irritates me most about men is...

52. I admire men who...

53. Men get angry when women...

54. Women dislike it when men act like...

55. I predict that women will...

56. A woman's hardest choice is...

57. Women can improve their situations by...

58. Women and men have in common...

59. A major issue between men and women is...

60. Women and men can communicate better by...

61. In a family, the woman should be responsible for...

62. A man's household responsibilities should include...

63. A weakness of men is...

64. An admirable trait of men is...

65. Women colleagues should treat each other with...

66. Women have been helped most by...

67. A well known woman leader I respect is...

68. I applaud men for...

69. Women are usually appreciated for...

70. Women have a right to...

71. I acknowledge that men are...

72. The advancement of women is hindered by...

73. Women and men can work together better by...

74. A pressing issue for many women is...

75. The advice I would give a young woman today is...

76. My opinion of men is...

77. People misinterpret feminism because...

78. Women are not informed about...

79. The most positive thing about men is...

80. If I could point out one thing to men, it would be...

81. Women are sometimes self conscious about...

82. Women should continue to...

83. Women should speak out about...

84. The most pressing issue women face is...

85. Women must not ignore the issue of...

86. Some women are angry because...

87. The reason some men resent women is...

88. An issue for women that needs to be re-examined is...

89. A stumbling block for many women is...

90. Women should request politicians to consider...

91. Men and women can help each other by...

92. The women's movement should be more vocal about...

93. An issue that women should clarify is...

94. Women's economic conditions could be improved by...

95. An upcoming important political issue for women is...

96. The direction of women's organizations must be...

97. A positive course of action for women is...

98. The women's movement can embrace the victory of...

99. Women can celebrate...

100. The lives of women and men can be enriched by...

CHAPTER FOUR

FIELD ASSIGNMENTS

These field assignments are designed to be completed outside of the classroom environment. Much of what women and men learn about each other is done through observations and personal experiences. The field assignments presented in this chapter cover areas such as generation issues, sex roles stereotypes, portrayal of women and men through novels and cards, and the messages men and women communicate by the way they dress and behave.

FIELD ASSIGNMENT ONE
WOMEN AND GENERATION

Develop a list of four questions and ask them to a woman in her twenties and a woman in her fifties or sixties. Compare and contrast their answers.

1.

2.

3.

4.

FIELD ASSIGNMENT TWO
RADIO LISTENING ACTIVITY

Listen to a morning radio program for twenty minutes. Listen for sex role stereotypes. Analyze the comments of the disc jockey, radio guests and listeners who call into the program and write a summary of your findings below:

92

FIELD ASSIGNMENT THREE
ROMANCE NOVEL REVIEW

Review a romance novel and answer the following questions:

1. **Give a physical description of the lead female character and the lead male character in the novel.**

2. **Describe the personality of this same lead female character and lead male character.**

3. **What physical and personality traits make these characters attractive?**

4. **Did the characters have any traits that made them unattractive?**

5. **How might a young adolescent girl interpret these characters?**

FIELD ASSIGNMENT FOUR
FRIENDHIP CARDS

Go to a local store and find two friendship or romantic cards. Analyze the written message and the art work or picture on the card.

1. Was the card degrading to either sex?

2. Compare the two cards on how they portray the roles of women and men.

3. Was there anything in the card that someone might find offensive? Explain your answer.

FIELD ASSIGNMENT FIVE
PEOPLE OBSERVATION

Go out and sit for a few minutes on a college campus or at a library or shopping mall. Observe two people, a man and a woman. Analyze the type of clothes the people are wearing and their behavior.

1. **What image was the woman trying to project by the clothes she wore and her behavior?**

2. **Did you feel the man's personality was accurately reflected by the clothes he wore? Explain your answer.**

3. **What are some things women and men communicate about themselves in the way they dress?**

FIELD ASSIGNMENT SIX
WORK OBSERVATION

Go into a local business and observe a male and a female worker. Identify who is in the supervisory role and who is working under him or her. Watch the interaction between the two workers and write a summary of your observations.

FIELD ASSIGNMENT SEVEN
FAMILY OBSERVATION

Observe a family who has both male and female children. You can observe a holiday family gathering, children playing at the park or in a store with their parents. Observe how the parents treat the children of the different sexes. Are the parents stricter or more lenient with one child more than the other? Give specific examples as you discuss your observations below:

FIELD ASSIGNMENT EIGHT

Interview an elementary age child and ask the first three questions below:

1. **What kind of work do you want to do when you grow up?**

2. **Why?**

3. **Do your parents work inside or outside of the home? What kind of work did they do?**

4. **Did the child pick an occupation similar to his or her parents? Yes or No? Explain the child's answer.**

FIELD ASSIGNMENT NINE
ANALYSIS OF A SONG

Listen to a song on the radio several times. Analyze how the lyrics of the song address women or men. Do the lyrics make assumptions about how women or men should behave? Write your observations below:

TITLE OF SONG:

OBSERVATIONS:

FIELD ASSIGNMENT TEN
SHOPPING OBSERVATION

Observe a young married couple in the grocery store. Write an observation of the couple in the space below. Consider things like who made the food selections. How did the couple decide the items they selected for the cart? Which spouse paid for the food?

CHAPTER FIVE

WRITING IN THE WORLD OF WOMEN'S STUDIES

If you go to the local bookstore, you will probably notice that women's studies books have increased in number over the years. Some bookstores now have a women's studies section that specializes totally in women's studies. With this new and renewed interest in women's studies, the door for writing opportunities has opened. Writing opportunities exist in all areas of women's studies and many academic fields address women's studies issues and concerns.

Writers in women's studies have different reasons for wanting to write books. Some writers want to educate the world about feminism and women. Almost every book I read on feminism has a new angle or philosophical approach to the subject. For others, writing in the area of women's studies has helped them put their past and future experiences in perspective. Writers in women's studies have also written books to explore policies, laws, management systems, and other concerns for women.

Whatever the reason, women's studies writers have something to say about women, and they want to share it with the readers. However, like writers in other fields, they have to find publishers and editors who are interested in their work and are willing to publish it. This book is written to help ease some of the pain for writers who are seeking to publish women's studies manuscripts.

Most beginning writers in women's studies have a number of questions about sending their articles and book manuscripts to publishers. The rest of this chapter is written in a question and answer format to help respond to questions that new writers might have about writing in the field of women's studies. I have tried to answer the questions in terms of the field of women's studies while being aware that the opinions of editors and publishers may vary from press to press.

How Do I Know If My Women's Studies Book Is Appropriate For A Publisher?

There are two ways to find out if your women's studies book is appropriate for a publisher. One way is to mail a query letter to the editor detailing your topic. The other way is to call the editors of publishing companies to talk with them. The query letter is somewhat more effective, because many editors do not want to or have time to take phone calls. Some publishing companies will not even transfer your call to an editor. They will simply send the writer submission guidelines. During the few times I have talked with editors, I have found they are very helpful in routing the manuscript to the right person.

The reason it is important to find out if your women's studies manuscript is appropriate for a publishing firm is to save you time and postage expenses. Many publishers will indicate they are interested in women's studies books. However, on closer examination, I find that some publishers only want very specific women's studies topics, such as women in history or story collections on women. Writers must search to find a women's studies publisher who specializes in the particular focus of their article or book.

What Are Some Examples Of Women's Studies Topics I Could Write About?

There are many broad topics and categories to write about in women's studies. For example, articles and books can be written about women in particular fields. Women in the medical field or women in literature or films may be one broad theme explored in women's studies. There are also writing opportunities to explore on philosophical questions and issues about feminism and sexism. Opportunities to write biographies on women's lives detail the paths and struggles women have faced. From a political standpoint, a writer can explore women's concerns related to government policies, laws, and program development. Social, psychological, and health concerns for women are also topics that continuously need to be explored. Within these broad categories are thousands of specific topics and ideas to write about and explore in women's studies. Writers may even have areas of expertise they want to build up and show strengths in the area of women's studies. For example, a high profile scientist may specialize in examining women in scientific fields.

How Long Should My Women's Studies Book Be In Length?

The length of the book will vary accordingly to the writing guidelines of women's studies publishers. I have seen women's studies books range from fewer than one hundred pages to as many as four hundred pages. I have noticed the length of pages in many cases is somewhere between seventy to two hundred and fifty pages. However, I have noticed in receiving information from one women's studies publisher that there was a requirement of a minimum of two hundred typed double-spaced pages. My advice is to write as many pages as it takes to adequately cover the women's studies topic. Be aware that an editor may cut out some of your work or ask you to expand on an idea to give the book a fuller meaning. There are times that a publisher may only want a particular section of a book. The publisher may decide to purchase only a chapter to use in another women's studies textbook or may select a story to use within a women's studies collection book. A women's studies writer may also have to decide if he or she is willing to break up a book.

How Long Will It Take An Editor To Respond To A Women's Studies Submission?

The length of response from a publisher is always a difficult question to answer because it is different with each publishing company and editor. Some publishing companies and university presses may have to send the manuscript to several reviewers for comments and recommendations. This can take several months or years. Other publishers take a two-step process where a manuscript goes through preliminary reviews before the final decision is made by an editorial board. Occasionally, an editor will call quickly after receiving the manuscript and will help keep the writer up-to-date on its progress. Publishing companies vary on length and response time. Some companies are very slow to respond, while others get back to the writer in a reasonable time. The dilemma for the writer is how long to wait for a publisher to make a decision before submitting the book manuscript to another publisher.

Should I Include A Resume When I Submit A Women's Studies Manuscript To A Publisher?

One editor I talked with on the phone asked me to include a resume. She told me that if the publisher liked the book and decided to offer me a contract, there would be information available for the editor to promote the writer. I think including a resume to an editor gives a profile of the writer's past accomplishments. If the editor knows something about the writer's educational and professional background, he or she will better understand the writer's angle and purpose for the book. It also helps if the writer is very specialized in the field that he or she is writing about. In most cases, a well written resume can add to the initial women's studies proposal that the writer is submitting to the publishing company. It might be just the thing to capture an editor's attention and cause him or her to read the book manuscript or article. The resume may also include a list of previous publications. Other publications and articles related to the theme of the book may add to the author's credibility.

Who Is The Audience For Women's Studies Books?

The general audience for women's studies books is broad and diverse. There are women who are exploring life's changes who read women's studies books in order to help them better cope with health, social, psychological, and aging issues they are facing in life. College students use and buy women's studies books as they are writing dissertations and researching information for term papers. College professors and researchers in many areas use women's studies books as they focus on topics related to and about women. Some women facing personal crises read women's studies books to help them face divorce, deal with career changes and goal settings, and to understand child care issues. The topics in women's studies are so broad that they interest a wide array of personalities and educational backgrounds for the audience of readers. Young and old readers are interested in different aspects of women's studies. In addition, women's studies books can be published at an international level to reach a variety of cultures.

What Is One Of The Best Ways For A Beginning Women's Studies Writer To Get Published In A Journal?

I think one of the best ways to get published in women's studies journals is to write a book review of a women's studies book. If you contact an editor of a women's studies journal, he or she may even send you a book to review. I reviewed a book that was sent to me by a women's studies editor and it became my first publication. I was hooked at that point and several book reviews followed in the later months. Once I knew I had the confidence to get a book review published, I then moved into longer journal articles and eventually to books. It was a process for me, but book reviews helped me to get my foot in the door and to understand journal publications. One advantage of journal publications is the time the editors have to help the beginning writer develop and improve his or her writing skills. Take advantage of the opportunities that any editor provides you in improving your writing skills. The feedback from journal editors can help beginning writers organize ideas and rethink how information can be phrased.

What Is The Advantage Of Publishing Women's Studies Articles In Journals?

One major advantage of being published in women's studies journals is to publicize research studies. Many women's studies graduate students are conducting research projects to complete requirements for master's and doctoral degrees. College professors and researchers are involved in a variety of research projects. Some doctoral programs at universities even require doctoral candidates to write a journal article so they can publish the results of the research. Publishing in a journal is not usually done for money. I have never been paid for journal articles that were published. There are even academic journals that require the author to pay for the pages in the journal once the article is accepted. Journals do provide good exposure for writers in the academic world. There are many journals that request articles about women and this is a beginning point for many women's studies writers. Some of the women's studies journals are student-focused and give opportunities for students to display their writings and essays about women. There are also women's studies journals that are sponsored by organizations and women's groups. A few journals are special editions or issues that focus on women's concerns and other feminist topics.

Am I More Likely To Get A Women's Studies Article Published If It Is Long And Extensive?

I used to think that the more time I spent writing a long and extensive article, the greater chance it had to be published in a journal or magazine. I soon found out that this was not necessarily true. One afternoon, during my lunch hour, I went to the university library. I spent about twenty minutes composing a short article. I mailed the brief article to a journal and it was published a month later. I wish I could say that journal articles were always this easy, but they are not. Some articles that I have spent much time writing and thinking about have never been published. Sometimes a writer must pick a topic that a journal editor is interested in publishing. I once wrote a journal article on American Indian women in higher education. The article was probably published because the journal needed articles on American Indian women and not too many people were writing on this subject. If you write a timely topic about women, it has a greater chance of being published, whether it is short or extensive.

Does A Rejection Letter From A Women's Studies Publisher Mean My Manuscript Is Rejected Forever?

Not necessarily, it depends on what the rejection letter conveys to you as the writer. Many rejection letters are form letters and some are postcards without an editor's signature. Once in a great while, the women's studies writer will receive a rejection letter with personal comments on the manuscript. This is a positive sign because an editor thought enough to respond with a personal letter. These suggestions can be helpful in rewriting and expanding the manuscript. In addition, you can later correspond with someone you have made contact with in the publishing company. An editor may become your contact person and may be seen as a step in the right direction toward a future publication. As many aspiring writers will tell you, "Do not overlook any personal comments or suggestions that an editor or publisher gives to you." It might lead to the road of a publication.

What Are Some Components Of An Effective Women's Studies Proposal?

Proposal guidelines will vary among women's studies publishers so always write for a copy of the guidelines. However, there are usually some common features in most proposals. Most publishers will want to see a short description that gives a summary of the book. The publisher may even want to know the estimated length of the women's studies manuscript and a time frame for completing the book. Many publishers will want you to look at competition from similar books and target unique aspects of the book for a specific audience. The proposal will usually include sample chapters of writing and a very extensive table of contents. The publisher will probably want to see a resume or vita to examine the writer's experience and credentials. Some writer's add other things to their proposals, such as writing samples or journal articles, information about personal appearances, workshops they have conducted, as well as other items to show the writer's expertise.

The following chapters include phrases on the topics of feminism, women's studies, sexism, the women's movement, and sex roles. These phrases can be adapted to many areas that students, scholars, and researchers write about as they study women in various fields. These phrases may be put into action in articles, essays, and reaction papers.

CHAPTER SIX

FEMINIST AND FEMINISM PHRASES

feminism spread during this period

the women held a feminist campaign

religious feminists had a somewhat different viewpoint

some feminists were angry

a feminist agenda was proposed

feminists rebelled against the idea of

feminism has been described many ways

strong emotions were expressed after the talk on feminism

the history of feminism emphasized

the development of the feminist movement

an example of an early feminist was

the feminist idea was

a cultural feminist said

feminist policy was developed

the feminist voted

social feminists worked towards

the feminist progress was facing roadblocks

the feminists were seeking to reach their goals

education was a key factor in helping feminism

there was a new wave of feminist thinking

problems were faced by the feminists

some women thought feminism was confusing

feminism can be seen as an ideology

the feminist culture was characterized

the feminist was inclined to

feminist research was important

feminist literature revealed

feminist issues were discussed

feminist scholars addressed the questions

a sociological feminist clarified the concerns

a feminist approach helped

the speaker presented a feminist perspective

a feminist theory was developed

feminist action was taken

there was criticism of feminism

a collection of feminist readings was presented

feminism was considered interdisciplinary

the principals of feminism were explained

a feminist consciousness was raised

a feminist methodology was proposed

feminist scholars gathered to

feminist scholarship was recognized

the feminists formed an organization

feminist therapy came into focus

the feminist philosophy questioned the

gender roles were discussed in the feminist lecture

feminist indoctrination began to

feminist values included

the feminist refused to accept

a new feminism seemed to come about

a humanistic feminist had an interesting perspective

the speaker was a contemporary feminist

the feminist objected to

the male feminist showed support

the biblical feminists shared their view

the activists marched for feminism

traditional homemakers viewed feminists as

the speaker was a liberal feminist

the feminist was quite bold

the group showed hostility to feminism

some of the feminist issues were abandoned

the feminists neglected to address

the lawmakers show a disinterest in feminist issues

the feminist effectively voiced concerns

the feminists took an academic approach

some of the feminist ideas were accepted

others welcomed the feminists to speak

some feminist measures were approved

a recognized feminist authored the report

the feminists endorsed the cause

the feminists were justified

many feminists were very committed

the feminists mustered up support for

some feminists were demanding

there was a rally supporting feminism

feminists joined together

the feminists collaborated

feminist concerns were studied

research on feminism found

a large group was in attendance at the first feminist rally

attention was given to feminist issues

emotions became strong about feminists

the struggle for feminism began when

the frame of mind of some feminists was

the feminists filled the auditorium

the support for feminism was well documented

a consciousness about feminism developed

there was some apprehension about feminism

the judgments made about feminism were somewhat harsh

feminism established benchmarks

some converted to feminism

there was astonishment about feminism

as feminists became stronger it puzzled some

disapproval by some groups was given to the feminists

feminists were criticized for their beliefs

feminists were frowned upon by some

the feminists brought up new challenges

there were roadblocks for feminism

feminism took bold strides

feminists became firm in their stand

strong steps were taken by feminists

the speaker was surprised at the reaction to the feminist topic

the feminist call was made

a request was made by feminists for

the center core of feminism was

the centralized issue of feminism was

the fight for feminism intensified

definite plans were made to strengthen feminism

feminism has been reshaped over the years

changes were made to modify feminism

feminism changed over time

certain things symbolized feminism

feminism was representative of

feminism was determined individually

there were positive attributes of feminism

others viewed feminism from a negative point of view

feminists decide what issues to take up

the circumstances surrounding feminism

the discussion on feminism lacked clarity

the feminist anticipated more change

a commentary was made on feminism

the typical response to feminism

not everyone was comfortable with the feminists

there were stereotyped ideas about feminists

the summary on feminism caused the audience to question

there was a strong attack on feminism

some grumbled as the feminists spoke

the issues of feminism became more complicated

deliberate efforts were made to help feminism

distinguished scholars spoke in favor of feminism

a considerable and noteworthy speech was made for feminism

feminism continued to change lives

the contention of feminists was to

the feminists showed endurance

the feminists had dialogue about the concerns

hearings allowed feminists to express their point of view

feminists generated interest on the topic

feminists were credited for

the ideas of feminism originated

some politicians praised feminists

other lawmakers were critical of feminists

the opposition had a faultfinding mission on the feminists

an analysis of views was conducted on feminism

feminists were scrutinized by the media

feminists were divided on the agenda

feminists helped instruct others

feminism was included in various curriculums

the public became more informed about feminism

people became curious about feminism

there was a desire to know more about feminism

feminists enlightened the press

patterns of thinking developed among feminists

there was voting on some feminists issues

feminism was distinguished from

the feminist movement was marked by

key elements of feminism were

feminism was opened up for interpretation

feminist terminology was confusing

the intensity of feminism increased

a narrative on feminism was presented

feminism started to have purpose

self-assurance developed from feminism

feminists showed great determination

feminists became more independent

feminists worked together with fortitude

it was concluded that feminists

the issues of feminism have not been resolved

new feminist concerns were uncovered

the progress of feminism seemed slow

feminism was spreading

feminists elaborated on key points

the growth of feminism was steady

some feminists deviated to other interests

at times feminism was wearisome

there was an eagerness to spread feminism

feminists were very capable

feminists were outspoken about certain things

feminists functioned in various occupations

others sponsored feminist activities

feminism spread through various regions

there was an international interest in feminism

there were some weaknesses in the feminist movement

some squabbled about feminism

there was some division among feminists

the expectations of feminism were

feminists searched for more information

feminists were watchful of

discrimination bothered feminists

the panel discussion was heated on feminism

quarrels abounded on the topic of feminism

there was a feminist symposium

arguments were common in feminist discussions

feminism stimulated discussion

there was an extreme dislike for feminists

some feminist groups disbanded

communication broke down among some feminists

feminism did not disappear

some were discouraged by feminism

feminists made some regrettable mistakes

feminists paid tribute to the early pioneers

prominent feminists helped recruit others

some of the misery of feminism came from

relationships changed because of feminism

feminism was a combination of things

there were some new issues coming out of feminism

feminism aggravated some people

many were opinionated about feminism

some wanted to dominate the feminists

some feminist issues remained unresolved

there was wavering among some feminists

feminists were visionary

feminists were steered in new directions

some people were indecisive about feminism

feminists had zeal for the cause

feminists approached the opposition fervently

there was a battle for feminists

change came about for feminists after the struggle

skilled leaders developed from feminism

feminists discussed some very practical issues

feminists were interested in economic issues

feminists had resiliency

feminists wanted to eliminate unfairness

feminists articulated their requests

feminists stressed ideas for solutions

there was some turmoil as feminists spoke out

some groups resented the feminists

others were oversensitive to feminist issues

the feminists ideas captivated some

feminists encountered negative responses

feminists remained optimistic in the cause

at times there was a revitalization of feminism

feminists received help and aid from

some lawmakers befriended feminists

feminists appreciated the reassurance from

celebrities began to endorse feminists issues

there was a strong sense of energy from the feminists

feminists felt pressure

feminists enjoyed sharing their views

the media helped to spread the word about feminism

feminist views stretched internationally

some people exaggerated feminist claims

feminism secured more support

some expressed humor about feminism

the group was devoted to feminist issues

feminism helped change living conditions for some

feminism opened a passage for

the threshold of feminism was

feminism is an on-going study

the essence of feminism was

feminism established many things

feelings were validated through feminism

feminism has endured

there were memorable moments from feminism

there was a heightened interest in feminism

feminists corresponded with

feminism was far reaching

branches of feminist organizations came about

feminists faced the confrontations

college students became familiar with feminism

the spotlight was on feminism

feminists were featured on television

a political awareness came from feminism

some feminists were forceful

the issues of feminism were overpowering

there was a clash of values at the feminist conference

the opponent was angry with the feminist

feminists accomplished an array of goals

feminists stood firmly

henceforth, people followed the feminists

the ground work was formed to address feminist issues

the fundamental ideas of feminism were in the report

feminists reunited to keep the cause on focus

feminism concentrated on various efforts

feminists compiled names of interested people

feminists delivered literature

feminists made remarkable steps

CHAPTER SEVEN

WOMEN'S STUDIES PHRASES

the philosophy of the women's studies program is

the terminology of the women's studies department

women's studies addressed changing societal needs

the women's studies program is interdisciplinary

there was scholarly activity in the women's studies program

there were changing priorities in the women's studies program

the women's studies division changed

there was a new vision from women's studies

therefore , the mission of the women's studies project is

the women's studies curriculum is aligned with

leadership is part of the women's studies program

women's studies is a cooperative effort

essential competencies were a part of the women's studies program

the objectives for the women's studies program

long range plans were developed for women's studies

women's studies short range goals are to

women's studies integrates the areas of

one strategy used in women's studies is

women speakers shared their experiences in women's studies

field trips added experiences to the women's studies program

the women's studies program incorporated

a multicultural focus was added to the women's studies program

the women's studies program encouraged different ethnic viewpoints

the outcomes of the women's studies department includes

the women's studies program gave a recap of

a description of the women's studies program was provided

the women's studies program was assessed by

a team reviewed the women's studies program

clear objectives were stated for women's studies

the women's studies program utilized

it was a designated women's studies program

resources were available to the women's studies program

presentations were made at the women's studies conference

the women's studies department submitted a written plan

a video library was established in the women's studies program

women's studies materials were reviewed

the faculty gained an appreciation of women's studies

the women's studies programs was distinguished from

the strength of the women's studies program is

several weaknesses were identified in women's studies

the women's studies program encouraged critical thinking

many opportunities were provided in women's studies

there were academic challenges in women's studies

the women's studies class was monitored

women's studies had an organized curriculum

the administration was supportive of women's studies

central themes were discussed in women's studies

interaction was encouraged in women's studies

after the evaluation changes were made in women's studies

improvement plans were made by the women's studies program

women's studies provided an exciting learning environment

women's studies classes enhanced understanding

students were active in the women's studies conference

women's studies faculty enlighten others at staff development

there were planned courses in women's studies

students kept writing logs in women's studies

portfolios were reviewed in women's studies

a school wide presentation was made by women's studies

a number of creative projects came from women's studies

women's studies developed a book sharing program

the academic focus of women's studies was

women's studies books were circulated to

the women's studies program was purposeful

women's studies became a year round program

student initiatives were developed in women's studies

women's studies developed procedures to

a women's studies display was used to show

new resources were ordered to update the women's studies department

women's studies had clear concise expectations

others acknowledged women's studies

women's studies was enhanced by the change

it was an inventive women's studies program

the women's studies program communicated the

the women's studies conference was accountable

interest in women's studies increased

the women's studies project demonstrated

enriching experiences were shared from women's studies

positive feedback was given in the women's studies program

women's studies criteria reflect

a sense of independence was felt from the women's studies program

the women's studies program targeted

women's studies faculty actively participated in the

purposeful dialogue came from the women's studies area

the women's studies program was highly criticized

women's studies became an international effort

the women's studies program was certified

serious questions were posed to the women's studies group

a women's studies guide was produced

students were advised about majoring in women's studies

women's studies began to educate others

the benefit of women's studies was realized

the women's studies project was revised

it was an ongoing women's studies project

the women's studies program was individualized

women's studies majors came from varied backgrounds

there were barriers in establishing a women's studies major

the women's studies department expanded

there were many possibilities for women's studies

the women's studies area was highly acclaimed

a directory of women's studies programs was developed

women's studies faculty had a brain storming session

the women's studies major was promoted on campus

a list of students interested in women's studies was generated

a library of women's studies research was organized

an outline showed the progress of women's studies

the women's studies program was shuffled around
women's studies was introduced to the campus
the contents of the women's studies program was presented
many things were incorporated in women's studies
women's studies majors produced an essay book
women's studies contributors shared at the forum
the format of women's studies was
a rough draft of the women's studies program was submitted
a marketing program helped promote women's studies
a cross-curriculum approach was used in women's studies
the women's studies department had an orientation
the procedures for declaring a women's studies major were
a fact book described the women's studies major
after the evaluation, the women's studies program began
a series of women's studies articles was published
grant proposals were developed from the women's studies project
the collection of women's studies writing was excellent
a magazine highlighted the women's studies program
a women's studies column was published in the newspaper
the women's studies area had a well organized major
women's studies kept track of its graduates
other departments took part in the women's studies function
advisors explained the women's studies major
several departments gave input to women's studies
women's studies was a small department
there were administrative changes in women's studies
women's studies was discontinued for lack of funds
a strong women's studies program was visualized

the current review of women's studies was positive

the theme of women's studies began to change

there was opposition of the women's studies program

the women's studies department addressed the concerns

the women's studies major was a forerunner in the field

women's studies provided the group historical information

concerns were handled by the women's studies program

the women's studies project applied for national grants

a donation provided needed funds for women's studies

the mission of women's studies was articulated

a successful women's studies major was implemented

new materials were delivered to the women's studies program

frequent dialogue was important in women's studies

faculty and students interacted about women's studies

leadership training improved women's studies

internships were provided for women's studies majors

fellowships provided teaching experiences in women's studies

graduate programs were offered to women's studies majors

a mentoring program was developed in women's studies

the principles of women's studies were addressed

there was gaining enrollment in women's studies

a strong commitment came from women's studies

women's studies identified a target area

a calendar of events was developed for women's studies

time was allocated for women's studies

outstanding practices in women's studies were recognized

women's studies took a cooperative approach

women's studies majors had problem solving experiences

there was broad participation in women's studies

the women's studies project had a wide range of events

the women's studies project focused on appreciation of

the unique aspects of women were discussed at the women's studies conference

women's studies participated with the coalition

issues were resolved with the help of women's studies

men were involved in the women's studies program

supervisory assistance was provided by women's studies

women's studies hosted the celebration

a women's studies advisory counsel was established

the morale was high in the women's studies department

a women's studies committee was formed

the women's studies program acted in a professional manner

there was a vested interest in women's studies

women's studies majors attended the state conference

community involvement helped the women's studies program

an information packet was developed for women's studies

a newsletter opposed women's studies

an open house for the women's studies program was planned

a women's studies center was built

a women's speaker club was developed as part of women's studies

press releases helped promote women's studies

personal letters were sent from women's studies

questionnaires were developed for opinions about women's studies

interim reports were sent from women's studies

the summative report praised women's studies

volunteers helped the women's studies event

college functions were assigned to women's studies

acceptance was gained in the women's studies program

progress reports gave a nice overview of women's studies

a statement was issued from the women's studies department

a designated faculty member represented women's studies

pertinent information came from the women's studies department

a women's studies play was presented

women's studies was specified as

the women's studies program was housed in

data was gathered on the women's studies major

the degree of support for women's studies was varied

the women's studies program was advised to

a reasonable effort was made to help women's studies

women's studies provided the appropriate documents

a final decision was made on funding women's studies

the women's studies major reflected the campus mission

a framework of courses was developed for women's studies

the department chair confirmed the report on women's studies

the women's studies program actively resolved concerns

the women's studies program was in compliance

the women's studies handbook was updated

the evaluation was stressful for women's studies

timelines helped organize the women's studies department

in-house data further explained the women's studies area

job descriptions were listed for women's studies

a multicultural faculty was recruited in women's studies

accountability was a chief concern in women's studies

adjunct faculty were hired for the women's studies department

the content of women's studies courses was reviewed

the women's studies department approved the textbooks

the women's studies department was reviewed periodically

delegates were assigned to the women's studies conference

the primary focus of women's studies is

an endowment was made to women's studies

the changing concepts of women's studies

several departments combined to form women's studies

a common belief about women's studies is

some researchers feel there is no agreement about women's studies

certain generalizations were made about women's studies

studying the past and present are part of women's studies

the women's studies department took a futuristic approach

women's studies entailed numerous concepts

the trend in women's studies programs is

the substance of the women's studies project was to

the program had an impact on the future of women's studies

the most critical question in women's studies concerns

women's studies programs facilitate the

an extensive report was presented on women's studies

the women's studies department integrated the program content

the dean's office provided guidance to the women's studies program

the underlying meaning in women's studies comes from

women's studies programs were opened up to analysis

life experiences had an impact in women's studies

activities reinforced the ideas of women's studies

women's studies majors were placed in practical settings

recognized professionals shared their experiences with women's studies majors

the outcomes of the women's studies project were promising

concerns were prioritized by the women's studies department
the importance of women's studies was downplayed by some
a series of lectures highlighted women's studies
some questioned the direction of women's studies
women's studies demonstrates the importance of
proponents of women's studies programs
many components make up women's studies
the attitudes of women's studies graduates were presented
one possible approach to women's studies
women's studies programs often ignore
a grasp was developed for women's studies
a pre-study was conducted on interest in women's studies
a blueprint was designed for the women's studies program
several required courses in women's studies include
curriculum committees created the women's studies program
a revised curriculum changed women's studies
students expressed their ideas about women's studies
women's studies developed a statement of beliefs
each phase of women's studies took a new direction
women's studies exhibits were presented at college fairs
social changes influenced women's studies programs
policies and procedures were shared in women's studies
the women's studies curriculum was flexible
scholarly activity was encouraged in women's studies
women's studies scholars started to forecast
women's studies has impacted other fields
the scope of women's studies serves as
implications for women's studies were discussed

there were several possible directions for women's studies

women's studies evolved from

ability levels varied among women's studies majors

women's studies continues to seek solutions

CHAPTER EIGHT

SEXISM PHRASES

the analysis of sexism

sexism raised issues about

research on sexism indicated

there are various problems related to sexism

one must define sexism

there are alternatives to sexism

the paper contained a discussion on sexism

sexism is even more complicated than

to recap sexism

programs are seeking to rid sexism

sexism overlaps with other forms of discrimination

the effects of sexism are long term

the article alerts colleagues about sexism

recent experiences suggest that sexism

one possible reaction to sexism

steps were taken to prevent sexism

it is a clear case of sexism

sexism continues to be investigated

a case presentation was made on sexism

it is frequently difficult to discuss sexism

there is intense emotion about sexism

sexism can result in painful feelings

there was heightened concern about sexism

a brief examination of sexism revealed

points to consider on sexism include

an example of sexism would be

the core problem of sexism is

sexism seems to be a worldwide phenomenon

there are many unreported cases of sexism

sexism puts professionals in difficult situations

brochures were prepared to combat sexism

sexism has been a tough battle

sexism was perceived as

attention was given to sexism

the feminists had grave concerns about sexism

there were heated talks on sexism

sexism was burdensome for many

sexism continues to affect lives

some were uncertain on how to handle sexism

sexism hinders progress

sexism is very frustrating

achievement was delayed by sexism

sexism interfered with equality

sexism hampered the balance in the workplace

qualified candidates were overlooked because of sexism

sexism was an obstacle to equilibrium

pay equivalence was crippled by sexism

reference was made to sexism

many people can recall incidents of sexism

there was evidence of sexism in small businesses

remarks were made with strong indications of sexism

sexism was implied in the paper

there were hints of sexism

the action insinuated sexism

the company announcement was evidence of sexism

the historical writing implied sexism

inferences were made to sexism

the case reminded others of how sexism is present

some occupations showed more cases of sexism

sexism inhibited upward mobility for some

the status of sexism is not clear

there were grounds for a sexism case

the paper on sexism was

sexism produced unevenness in the work environment

sexism is improper and out of place

life would be improved if sexism was gone

episodes involving sexism still exist

sexism caused setbacks

the influence of sexism influenced young thinkers

sexism infringed on the rights of

some became infuriated by sexism

sexism enraged those treated unfairly

descriptions of sexism were given

the arguments against sexism were

a proposal to address sexism was submitted

cases of sexism were questioned

on probing into sexism

investigations found sexism existed

the report disclosed sexism

sexism stirred up resentment

sexism affected job promotions

career advancement was hurt by sexism

some companies felt obligated to check into sexism

a diary contained a writing on sexism

the journalist explained an incident of sexism

there was a new awareness of sexism

educating the public helped in understanding sexism

efforts were made to resolve sexism

sexism became common place

employers began to address sexism

the management investigated reported cases of sexism

morale was down because of sexism

could there be an end to sexism

sexism endangered careers

the dilemma of sexism is

some owners would not address sexism

groups bolstered together to fight sexism

many clubs banded together to voice concerns on sexism

it took fortitude to take a stand on sexism

there were discussions about fairness in sexism

the essence of sexism

essentially sexism was described as

at the heart of sexism is

primarily, sexism can be explained by

testimony confirmed cases of sexism

cases were analyzed for elements of sexism

some ideas about sexism were misrepresented

an inquiry into sexism found

researchers explored how sexism was defined

a re-examination of sexism was needed

surveys were issued to gain information on sexism

examples of sexism were described at the forum

researchers exchanged ideas on sexism

investigating sexism became exhausting

a preliminary plan helped address issues of sexism

management checked all cases of possible sexism

workers scrutinized how companies handled sexism

sexism was widespread

fairness issues were important in evaluating sexism

the fallacy of sexism was

after the public became familiar with sexism

professionals were overwhelmed when sexism became an issue

companies denied wrongdoing in the area of sexism

a newspaper article called attention to sexism

sexism was the feature story in a local newspaper

to combat sexism a plan was developed

some workers did not speak out against sexism

fear of losing a job kept many silent about sexism

sexism was brought to light by

once sexism was exposed of

government agencies began to investigate sexism

the following is an example of sexism

to illustrate sexism the speaker explained

a case of sexism was pointed out

some employees were badgered by sexism

the cases of sexism were astounding

sexism was starting in the workplace

coalitions rallied against sexism

talking about sexism stirred up anger

there is a need to educate about sexism

a committee review of sexism found

appropriate changes were recommended to alleviate sexism

people interpreted their ideas about sexism

it is essential to understand the causes of sexism

sexism was viewed in a cultural content

there were long term implications from sexism

strategies were discussed to deal with sexism

there were some immediate effects of sexism

an alternative to sexism is

literature addressed concerns about sexism

the discussion on sexism was divided into strands

patterns of behavior influenced sexism

sexism emerged in a variety of settings

the group answered questions on sexism

the meaning conveyed by sexism

some did not comprehend sexism

sexism was communicated through different means

it is crucial for students to understand the hurt of sexism

sexism is abusive

sexism became a global issue

respect is part of dealing with sexism

ideas were exchanged about sexism

looking at past events helped explain sexism

cultural traditions impacted sexism

students were taught to respond objectively to sexism

different cases of sexism were studied

writings were analyzed for different aspects of sexism

a study compared the incidents of sexism

the value of workers was questioned by the case of sexism

sexism was discussed in a Sociology class

a workshop on sexism was offered

sexism was discussed in relation to racism

great literary pieces were analyzed for elements of sexism

a variety of writings illustrated sexism

the class on sexism revealed counseling strategies to help

the report described ways to reduce sexism

a plan was developed to help others cope with sexism

procedures were identified for dealing with sexism

factors that contribute to sexism were identified by

information on sexism was linked to other campuses

a formal publication on the topic of sexism was

students interacted verbally about sexism issues

sexism was compared and contrasted to

details were added to the report on sexism

ideas were brainstormed to eliminate sexism

sexism was related through the participants life experiences

the audience asked questions about sexism

sexism was described in a series of events

sexism generated many concerns

there was a constructive response for dealing with sexism

several methods were employed to counter sexism

multimedia resources were used to show sexism

several examples of sexism were stated

book presentations were made on sexism

a participant emphasized how sexism changed her life

sexism was rephrased to help explain the idea

information was required to see sexism issues

each case of sexism was classified

a network of resources was developed on sexism

the libraries located information on sexism

authors recognized sexism in stories

folktales were retold that showed sexism

a book review explained sexism

sexism was described in a telephone interview

information on sexism was organized

appropriate strategies were used to fight sexism

the stands of sexism were interlinked

confidence was developed to deal with sexism

the problems in sexism were restated

discussions on sexism were expanded to include

sexism was simplified so that

real life problems were related to sexism

sexism was connected to

the views of sexism were verified by

the discussion reflected the seriousness of sexism

some work diligently for solutions to sexism

an open-minded approach was taken to sexism

the resources were combined to battle sexism

sexism was expressed through written reports

students compared events on sexism

sketches were drawn to illustrate sexism

the feelings of sexism were explored

dramatizations showed sexism

pictures showed how sexism was portrayed

poems were read expressing feelings of sexism

sexism was put in another context

meaning was inferred to sexism

data was recorded and collected on sexism

awareness was the theme of the sexism conference

predictable patterns were investigated in sexism

sexism's impact on society could be seen

personal feelings were related about sexism

people had distinct definitions of sexism

it was an opinionated film on sexism

some paid the cost for sexism

treatment of individuals was a key issue in sexism

sexism became distorted

there was a major confrontation on sexism

standards for dealing with sexism emerged

sexism was examined in different geographic locations

faculty members made major contributions on sexism

group talks opened up discussions on sexism

sexism was observed through several avenues

groups worked cooperatively on dealing with sexism

a tentative list of subjects showed interest in the topic of sexism a detailed thesis was displayed on sexism

the crowd showed a willingness to discuss sexism

young students became aware of sexism and its' issues

the myths of sexism were discussed in the paper

teams worked collaboratively on the concept of sexism

persistence helped in addressing sexism

students and faculty served on the committee on sexism

a comparative study on sexism gave new insight

the usage of sexism phrases was explored

sexism was discussed on an executive level

different perspectives on sexism were presented

it took courage to stand up to sexism

the causes of sexism were evaluated

there was respect for the differing opinions on sexism

positive alternatives to sexism were presented

an exhaustive list of options to sexism was presented

innovative ideas came from the sexism conferences

research reports were shared on sexism

the prevailing view of sexism is

faculty presented numerous aspects of sexism

puppets helped teach about sexism

interpreting stories helped show how sexism existed

a chart was drawn to show the path of sexism

students responded to written cases on sexism

after sexism was defined, the examples were given

the class was divided into groups to explore sexism

a panel of students showed various viewpoints on sexism

important historical figures who spoke against sexism were

stories were adapted to show why sexism should not exist

a collage showed the theme of sexism

students examined the future of sexism

letters to government officials expressed concerns for sexism

a planned curriculum was presented on sexism

sexism was decreased following the implementation of

CHAPTER NINE

WOMEN'S MOVEMENT PHRASES

conflicts and problems plagued the women's movement

the women's movement opened doors

some women abandoned the women's movement

a woman was ostracized for speaking at the women's movement

many women absorbed the message of the women's movement

some took an academic approach to the women's movement

the women's movement endured because of

people started to acknowledge the women's movement

much was achieved through the women's movement

the women's movement made people realize that

the women's movement put across new ideas

the women's movement fulfilled a purpose

the women's movement produced

there were triumphs from the women's movement

the women's movement created opportunities

one victory for the women's movement was

a message was delivered from the women's movement

part of the success of the women's movement came from

the women's movement made numerous accomplishments

some professionals gave a nod of approval to the women's movement

the women's movement was applauded by

politicians became acquainted with the women's movement

the women's movement spread across the country

the women's movement proposed

the agenda of the women's movement was to

some questioned the actions of the women's movement

earnings became one issue of the women's movement

the reactions varied to the women's movement

energy came from the women's movement

a combined effort spurred on the women's movement

the women's movement formally addressed

there were also informal speeches in the women's movement

the women's movement reinforced

an extension of the women's movement was

stories were related to the women's movement

many testimonials were given in support of the women's movement

the women's movement indicated

the women's movement uncovered

not everyone had high regard for the women's movement

it was assumed the women's movement would

the women's movement worked for the betterment of

the women's movement pushed ahead

pressure on the women's movement found

the women's movement heralded

the women's movement proclaimed

warnings came from the women's movement

the women's movement provided encouragement

teaching others became part of the women's movement

the women's movement urged

women's movement reviewed facts

advocates were strong in the women's movement

inventive strategies were used in the women's movement

new topics arose from the women's movement

the pursuit of the women's movement was

various occupations were addressed in the women's movement

the intriguing aspect of the women's movement was

other organizations concurred with the women's movement

subsequent to the women's movement

contrary to the women's movement

a disruptive part of the women's movement came when

some saw the women's movement as threatening

the plan of the women's movement was

the women's movement had intentions for

some people drifted away from the women's movement

individuals participated in the women's movement

the women's movement suggested alternate ways to

many things evolved from the women's movement

the women's movement increased

women's movement was on the verge of

the astonishing thing about the women's movement was

the women's movement became goal-oriented

the women's movement had strong aspirations

the women's movement became aggressive

the output in the women's movement was

it was reported the women's movement

the women's movement used the media to

the women's movement was interpreted in many ways

the women's movement stated their requests

the hope of the women's movement was

the intuition of the women's movement

the women's movement made a reasonable request

the women's movement became highly visible

the women's movement gave the appearance of

the women's movement was utilized to

the women's movement designated

empowerment came from the women's movement

some individuals had gratitude for the women's movement

the women's movement was credited for

the arguments for the women's movement were

an open exchange characterized the women's movement

a schedule of events helped organize the women's movement

the shape of the women's movement

the women's movement represented different age groups

some disputes were resolved with support from the women's movement

concerns were verbalized through the women's movement

progress in the women's movement was hindered by

the women's movement acted as

new ground was broken by the women's movement

questions were posed by the women's movement

some individuals rallied for the women's movement

the women's movement united to address

the women's movement theorized

people speculated about the women's movement

one could surmise about the women's movement

researchers postulated about the future of the women's movement some people stood back and judged the women's movement

there was some bewilderment about the women's movement

the women's movement divided on some issues

opponents tried to block the success of the women's movement

the women's movement encountered

at the onset of the women's movement

the women's movement gave the appearance of

many were diligent about the women's movement

a seriousness came from the women's movement

the women's movement drew interest

the women's movement was audible

a clear message was sent from the women's movement

the women's movement created a sense of awareness

the women's movement was recognized for

the women's movement fostered

the women's movement was a champion for many causes

the women's movement promoted

the ideas maintained by the women's movement include

assistance was provided by the women's movement

the women's movement promoted

there was sustained interest in the women's movement

the women's movement was strengthened by

assertions were made by the women's movement

the women's movement was seriously criticized

the women's movement negotiated with

the women's movement faced barriers

there were hurdles for the women's movement

the women's movement was founded to

an important source to the women's movement

the groundwork for the women's movement came from

leaders in the women's movement reasoned

the women's movement strove to

the women's movement forged ahead

the women's movement made a loud statement

in view of the women's movement

the women's movement shifted

the women's movement established

the women's movement planted the seed for

attitudes were changed from the women's movement

the women's movement was praiseworthy of

a profile was developed on the women's movement

a history emerged on the women's movement

the women's movement blasted

the women's movement was summarized by

individuals bonded through the women's movement

the women's movement brought out

the widespread approach of the women's movement

faculty researched the women's movement

individuals expressed their feelings on the women's movement

predictions were made about the women's movement

the women's movement crusaded for

part of the women's movement campaign was to

help was solicited for the women's movement

college campuses share information in the women's movement

the women's movement grasped

the women's movement concentrated its efforts on

the women's movement made some blunders

in celebration of the women's movement

the women's movement was attacked on all sides

the women's movement changed thinking

diversification was part of the women's movement

some people had a narrow view of the women's movement

the setting for the women's movement was

the women's movement charged others with

the make-up of the women's movement was

the chief purpose of the women's movement

the women's movement looks at deep-seated issues

the women's movement circulated information about

the women's movement had purpose behind its actions

the women's movement coexisted with

the consistency of the women's movement was

the contemporary women's movement

the women's movement represented a combination of concerns

the women's movement came forward with

a compelling part of the women' s movement was

the women's movement managed to

the women's movement commenced to

comments were made about the women's movement

the women's movement responded to negative remarks

the women's movement was compared to

one thing that identified the women's movement was

the women's movement complained about

there was competition within the women's movement

the women's movement discovered some complex issues

some issues were twisted in the women's movement

the women's movement tried to untangle the

mixed emotions cropped up in the women's movement

the women's movement was perplexed by

a hampered women's movement bounced back

the women's movement addressed dilemmas

the women's movement leader had composure

the women's movement was wedged between

a central point of the women's movement

women clustered together for the women's movement

a concise response was given by the women's movement

in conjunction with the women's movement

a consequence of the women's movement

a consideration of the women's movement was

the women's movement was a consolidation of

the women's movement held a conference

there was a debate about the women's movement

notes were compared about the women's movement

the essence of the women's movement was

the women's movement reacted to many battles

the women's movement was a continuation of

the women's movement dovetailed

the same concerns were repeated in the women's movement

each struggle in the women's movement opened doors

the major contribution of the women's movement

money was contributed to the women's movement

there was a well-planned seminar on the women's movement

the women's movement assisted

the women's movement managed to influence

it was an opportune time for the women's movement

some contradicted the women's movement

there were different variations in examining the women's movement

the women's movement served

the women's movement devised a way to

informal talks were popular in the women's movement

people expressed their views of the women's movement

the women's movement was persuasive

correspondence came from the women's movement

counsel was provided to the women's movement

the creation of the women's movement came from

the women's movement crossed boundaries

the crossroads of the women's movement

cultural issues were raised from the women's movement

the women's movement questioned some customs

the women's movement showed evidence of

the pros and cons of the women's movement were discussed

the women's movement proclaimed

decisions were made because of the women's movement

one can conclude from the women's movement that

new terminology came from the women's movement

individuals commented about the women's movement

the women's movement was broad

the women's movement dispatched a clear message

a determined message came from the women's movement

the women's movement deviated from

aside from the women's movement

154

devoted leaders helped the women's movement

the magnificent part of the women's movement was

dignity was a result of the women's movement

the women's movement was an earnest effort

careful review of the women's movement found

the straightforward approach of the women's movement

the drawbacks of the women's movement

workers undertook assignments in the women's movement

ideas clashed about the women's movement

the women's movement stirred conflicts

there was an uneasiness about the women's movement

some discarded the ideas of the women's movement

there was bickering about the women's movement

some officials did not want to be approached about the women's movement

misunderstandings resulted from the women's movement

some aspects of the women's movement were distressing

the women's movement addressed aspects of equal rights

the women's movement disclosed

domestic issues were discussed in the women's movement

many individuals donated time to the women's movement

the women's movement executed

ambiguity was part of the women's movement

individuals had strong convictions about the women's movement

the women's movement eagerly met the challenges

the women's movement was a strenuous effort

the women's movement hungered for change

the women's movement elaborated on

the women's movement maintained

a forceful approach was taken by the women's movement

the women's movement articulated steps for change

the women's movement enabled women to

new changes were enacted from the women's movement

the women's movement was embellished by

celebrities pledged to help the women's movement

there were ardent supporters of the women's movement

the women's movement addressed work issues

the women's movement was an elaborate attempt to

an inquest into the women's movement

leaders in the women's movement were quoted

early writings from the women's movement

the women's movement faced limitations

the jargon of the women's movement

the newspaper had a commentary on the women's movement

the informative report described the women's movement

the meaningful side of the women's movement

at times the women's movement was dramatic

different branches of the women's movement developed

at times the women's movement seemed extreme

some saw the women's movement as an attempt to

various measures were addressed in the women's movement

some issues were vague in the women's movement

the fascination of the women's movement is

some were repelled by the women's movement

the women's movement pointed to

the spotlight was on the women's movement

a prominent figure in the women's movement was

the firm stance of the women's movement

the women's movement encountered new frontiers

the fundamental points addressed by the women's movement

the utmost concern of the women's movement was

the women's movement issues were explained in everyday terms

the strength of the women's movement was unrivaled

the grandeur of the women's movement was

CHAPTER TEN

SEX ROLE PHRASES

sex role development starts

sex role behaviors were witnessed

observations were made of sex role behaviors

sex role behavior was observed while students interacted

researchers postulated about sex roles

sex role attitudes

sex role behavior was identified

a study on sex roles revealed

there were cultural differences in the sex roles

there was confusion about sex roles

sex role mannerisms came from

sex roles were perceived as

sex role identity

sex role stereotypes can be seen in

different perspectives were found in sex role research

researchers speculated about sex roles

habits were examined in sex role research

play was important in studying children's sex roles

the presentation on sex roles

parents helped observe the sex role behavior

teachers gave numerous examples of sex role behavior

college students made sex role observations

sex role research is needed for

researchers collaborated to understand sex role stereotypes

information was shared about sex role identity

attitudes have changed about sex roles

dual career families have impacted sex roles

the significance of sex role research

understanding sex role development

sex role research can benefit

the contributions of sex role research

sex role studies contribute to

the advantage of sex role research is

sex role investigation is essential for

sex role understanding is instrumental for

the crucial aspect of sex role research is

an observational approach was used in the sex role study

sex role development is hindered by

there are preconceived ideas about sex roles

reference was made to sex roles

observations were made of sex role stereotypes

there was evidence of sex role stereotyping

a historical look at sex roles found

writings about sex roles revealed

sex role research signified

sex role behavior was recorded

records were kept documenting sex role behaviors

considerable importance was given to sex role research

sex role investigation was noticed

sex role images were investigated

sex role research was approached at different angles

the researcher's intuition about sex roles

researchers probed into understanding sex roles

sex role behavior was checked monthly

literature was examined on sex roles

a film depicted sex role stereotypes

there was an inquiry into sex role literature

a reviewer recorded data in the sex role study

data was collected immediately on sex roles

the sex role research symbolized

the hidden meaning of sex roles

the sex role researcher hinted at

another possible explanation for the sex role behavior

the implication of the sex role research was

advances were made in understanding sex role behavior

sex role research regenerated interest in

the researcher's sex role study was practical

a useful aspect of sex role research was

the sex role study elaborated on

errors were made in the sex role study

the limitations of the sex role research were

a grant funded the sex role study

the university gave support for a project on sex roles

subjects were given incentives for participating in the sex role study

the sex role research study was contrary to

an indicator of sex role attitudes

a unique aspect of sex role research is

the child displayed unusual sex role mannerisms

researchers were perplexed by the sex roles

the sex roles research study continued for several years

sex role research was initiated from

the proposed sex roles study brought attention to

sex role investigations were inspired by

sex role research took place in a day care center

there were problems with the sex role studies

sex role research was introduced by

the researcher's starting point for the sex role study was

observers practiced watching the sex role behavior in a pilot study

a sex role pre-test was given

researchers were surprised at the sex role attitudes

there was an intrusion in the sex role study

in view of the sex role research

subjects actively participated in the sex role study

the sex role study focused on young children

the sex role research contained too much jargon

it was a joint sex role study

the sex role study was in conjunction with

sex role research was justified by

the knowledge provided by sex role research was

helpful facts resulted from the sex role study

the published sex role study

a precedent was set with the sex role research

there was a lack of research on sex roles

sex role research crossed disciplines

groundwork was conducted prior to the sex role research

sex roles were examined at different age levels

a shortcoming of the sex role article was

verbal exchanges were analyzed for sex role information

students wrote essays on sex roles

sex role researchers maintained the idea that

funds were limited for sex role research

some administrators viewed sex role research as unimportant

the research assistant observed a student in the sex role study

a checklist was used to mark sex role behavior

researchers had weekly meetings on sex roles

the sex role research was a model for

the family was explored in the sex role research

sex role behavior was classified by

the study began with a review of articles on sex roles

women's groups commented on the sex role research

a required workshop was conducted on sex roles

students chose different aspects of sex role research to

mandatory sex role training was given

a compelling part of the sex role study was

changing sex role attitudes were

more research is needed on sex roles

several departments supported the sex role research

researchers conferred on the sex role findings

a criticism of sex role research was

sex role research drew disapproval

complaints were made about the sex role research

assistance was given on the sex role project

a series of investigations were conducted on sex roles

the researcher's opinions about sex roles were shared

a notion about sex roles is

the sex role class looked at different viewpoints

inferences were made about sex roles

the inclination about sex roles is

the method used to conduct the sex role research was

sex role research has been conducted many ways

sex role research is primarily conducted to

sex role research is related to

different grade levels were examined for sex role behavior

it was a fresh approach to sex role investigations

sex role researchers recorded the sex role behavior firsthand

extra data was generated from the sex role study

sex role data was correlated with

an interesting factor commenced in the sex role research

a startling discovery came from the sex role study

the framework of sex role research was

permission was obtained to do the sex role research

the playground was the setting for the sex role project

the pragmatic side of sex role research was

several researchers quoted the sex role study

the mission of the sex role research was

an academic question was posed about sex roles

curiosity developed about sex roles

a sex role questionnaire was developed

feedback was given about sex roles

papers were written on the topic of sex roles

the reaction was mixed to the sex role study

the sex role research was feasible

the social aspects of sex roles were highlighted

the traditional view of sex roles

there was ambivalence about sex roles

essays on successful careers were analyzed for sex role behavior

recommendations were made about sex roles

research assistants perceived the sex role study differently

the university reconsidered the sex role study

the sex role investigation was revamped

sex role attitudes of college students were compared to

a reflection on sex roles

sex role behavior was concentrated in one area

there was an association between sex roles and

the other side of sex roles concerns

new questions were formed from the sex role research

there was some reluctance about the sex role research

renewed interest was developed in sex roles

the dean supported the sex role research project

a follow-up sex role study was needed to

sex roles were viewed in a sequence of events

sex role behaviors were scored for

the sex role study continued for

there was some bias in the sex role study

the subject's sex role stereotypes were revealed in interviews

the researcher's prejudice was seen in the sex role study

a clear picture of sex roles was described

examples provided additional information on sex roles

students were unaware of their sex role behaviors

sex role research spread to other academic areas

sex role behavior was taken for granted

a typical sex role attitude for children is

the theoretical side to sex role research is

academically, sex role research is viewed as

a worthy study was contributed to understanding sex roles

unexpected results came from the sex role project

it was difficult to analyze the results of the sex role study

some aspects of sex roles were unexplored

there were doubts about the sex role research

the area of sex role research was unnoticed

sex role behavior continues to be explored

the future of sex role research is

BIBLIOGRAPHY

For gaining a better understanding of the issues that women and men face. The following books are suggested for reading:

Allen, Patricia. *Getting to "I Do."* New York, NY: William Morrow and Company, 1994.

Carter, Steven and Sokol, Julia. *Men Like Women Who Like Themselves (And Other Secrets that the Smart Women Know).* New York, NY: Delacorte Press, 1996.

Cutter, Rebecca. *When Opposites Attract: Right Brain/Left Brain Relationships and How They Work.* New York, NY: A Dutton Book, 1994.

Denfeld, Rene. *The New Victorians: A Young Woman's Challenge to the Old Feminist Order.* New York, NY: Time Warner, 1995.

Denfeld, Rene. *Kill the Body, The Head Will Fall: A Closer Look at Women, Violence and Aggression.* New York, NY: Time Warner, 1997.

Gray, John. *Mars and Venus on a Date.* New York, NY: Harper Collins, 1997.

Hudson, Pat. *The Solution-Oriented Woman: Creating the Life You Want.* New York, NY: W.W. Norton and Company, 1996.

Kelton, Nancy Davidoff. *Writing From Personal Experience: How to Turn Your Life Into Salable Prose.* Cincinnati, Ohio: Writer's Digest Books, 1997.

INDEX

ABOUT THE AUTHOR

Dr. Susan Louise Peterson is the author of *The Changing Meaning of Feminism: Life Cycle and Career Implications from a Sociological Perspective.* Her writings also include published articles on the topic of women in higher education. She has worked extensively with single parents and was named to the Practitioners' Hall of Fame for her contributions leading to the improvement of educational practice. Dr. Peterson has taught numerous college courses on how women and men communicate in the field of human relations.